Please return/re

...ATH & NORTH EAST

D1350988

1 1 0207067 0

BLOOD, TIN, STRAW

Satan Says
The Dead and the Living
The Gold Cell
The Sign of Saturn: Poems 1980–1987
The Father
The Wellspring

BLOOD, TIN, STRAW

Sharon Olds

CAPE POETRY

Published by Jonathan Cape 2000

2 4 6 8 10 9 7 5 3 1

First published in Great Britain in 2000 by
Jonathan Cape
Random House, 20 Vauxhall Bridge Road,
London SW1V 2SA

Random House Australia (Pty) Limited
20 Alfred Street, Milsons Point, Sydney,
New South Wales 2061, Australia

Random House New Zealand Limited
18 Poland Road, Glenfield,
Auckland 10, New Zealand

Random House (Pty) Limited
Endulini, 5A Jubilee Road, Parktown 2193, South Africa

The Random House Group Limited Reg. No. 954009
www.randomhouse.co.uk

Versions of 'The Promise' and 'The Prepositions' originally appeared
in *The New Yorker*. Other poems in this work were originally published in
the following publications: *American Poetry Review, The Atlantic Monthly,
Field, Fugue, The Gettysburg Review, Grand Street, Green Mountain Review,
Ironwood, Michigan Quarterly Review, Ontario Review, The Paris Review,
Ploughshares, Poetry, Poetry East, Poetry Ireland, The Quarterly, River Styx,
Salmagundi, Southern Review, Threepenny Review, TriQuarterly, VIAS –
Visions International, Washington Square Review, The Woodstock Journal.*

Heartfelt thanks to the Lyndhurst Foundation and to the Lila
Wallace-Reader's Digest Fund.

A CIP catalogue record for this book
is available from the British Library

ISBN 0 224 06089 9

Papers used by Random House are natural,
recyclable products made from wood grown in sustainable forests;
the manufacturing processes conform to the environmental
regulations of the country of origin

Typeset by Palimpsest Book Production Limited,
Polmont, Stirlingshire
Printed and bound in Great Britain by
Creative Print and Design (Wales), Ebbw Vale

For Bobbie and Galway

CONTENTS

Blood

Tin

Straw

Fire

Light

BLOOD

THE PROMISE

With the second drink, at the restaurant,
holding hands on the bare table,
we are at it again, renewing our promise
to kill each other. You are drinking gin,
night-blue juniper berry
dissolving in your body, I am drinking Fumé,
chewing its fragrant dirt and smoke, we are
taking on earth, we are part soil already,
and wherever we are, we are also in our
bed, fitted, naked, closely
along each other, half passed out,
after love, drifting back
and forth across the border of consciousness,
our bodies buoyant, clasped. Your hand
tightens on the table. You're a little afraid
I'll chicken out. What you do not want
is to lie in a hospital bed for a year
after a stroke, without being able
to think or die, you do not want
to be tied to a chair like your prim grandmother,
cursing. The room is dim around us,
ivory globes, pink curtains
bound at the waist – and outside,
a weightless, luminous, lifted-up
summer twilight. I tell you you do not
know me if you think I will not
kill you. Think how we have floated together
eye to eye, nipple to nipple,
sex to sex, the halves of a creature
drifting up to the lip of matter
and over it – you know me from the bright, blood-
flecked delivery room, if a lion
had you in its jaws I would attack it, if the ropes
binding your soul are your own wrists, I will cut them.

3

THE GIFT

If I could change one physical thing
about myself, I would retract those tiny
twilit lips which appeared at the mouth
of my body when the children's heads pressed out, I would
haul back up into heaven those little
ladder-tatters, although in the crush
between the babies' skull-plates and the skin
of the birth-gates, we want the symphysis
more cherished – and he seems to like those bruised
celestial wattles, their clasp, their tip-of-
seraph-pinion purple. They are
the last licks that the other world took,
crown to sole, along each darling,
he kisses a god's small tongues in them
and they soul-kiss him back. I think he could
make peace with a scar, if my breast were to be
cut out to save me, honor his way
along that seam, I think he could love me
if I had no body – did he love me before
he knew me, before I was born? Maybe
his love drew me to earth, my head
moved toward the surface of my mother's body
and the minuscule hands of her labia
midwived me out, I came toward him in her ribbons, through her
    favours.

ANIMAL MUSIC

The first time, my eyes were closed.
They seemed to have gone down deep into my body
and opened, there, seeing the coursing
bonfire colour in the torso. For those moments,
it felt as if there were an army inside me,
maybe at the second when the parted walls
of the Red Sea closed, again, with their shining
clasping closings. Then I was weeping on him,
and it began again, and my eyes opened,
and there was his temperate, serious face
in all its crisp visibleness,
whisker and eyelash – and if each time
is a song sung to one's love, I sang
to the outer curve of his iris. I love resting on him,
dark rest, on the staff line, then I
love to feel it mount, again,
from the base of matter. My eyes were closed,
I was in the flesh, I felt that I was
the blaze of the pressed, closed eye,
I lifted my lids an instant and shut them and had
gathered a glimpse of him, which glowed now
inside my eyelids, it was navy-blue of skin,
its lashes and lips a murked, straw-fire
gold, I sang to that image of him,
the fugue of those long instants the suffused
life-mask of my beloved. And then I looked at him,
then I would not look away from him,
the bristled, salt cheer of his face,
its absence of unkindness, and that wordlessness
which awes me, I sang to him, and rested, and sang to him,
the kisses wrenched
only by the wrying
of coming, the gazes skinned and skewed

only by it. But when I came to the end with him,
my eyes turned and sank, and the orbs of the eyeballs
and the optic nerve and the occipital lobe and the
earth-gemmery of the iris became
flesh of the rosy flesh of the cunt and
columnar throat – their convulsions
its convulsions, their night its night, their
sleep its sleep, their dream of love
its waking dream.

THE DEFENCE

When I walked into the seminar room
with my dissertation, our son floated in out
before me, treaded water in,
almost nine months old, upside-
down, sucking his thumb. My advisor
had called my thesis original,
richly metaphorical, and so
free of footnotes – I secretly thought
I might win something. But he didn't show up,
and the Chair of the Department had a pillar of mail
and a wastebasket down by his leg – for two hours,
he disembowelled. Two other men were
muttering to each other out the sides of their mouths,
and doing their hard *har, har,*
har. I cited my advisor for his
encouragement, I described the yards
of file cards, the research, but after five minutes of their
jokes and smirks, I saw that they meant
to flunk me. I drew my powers together,
120 pounds of me,
40 of the pregnancy
and 7 of my baby. Two hours later,
they asked me to leave the room for an interval
and they voted: Fail, Fail, Fail,
Fail, and You Can't *Do* That –
the one woman. When I lumbered back in,
our son's sweet palate may have wrinkled up
at the taste of fear's sour effluent –
who was polluting his waters? (Rip)
They wanted (Rip) a dissertation
absolutely new, without one
word (Rip) of this one – except
'the' was all right, and 'and'. How much

time shall we give her, gentlemen? How about
– nine months?! *Har, har,*
har. My cervix bent, for a moment,
with intimate, private hurt. I said,
Thank you. I thought, if you have hurt my child with that,
if you have curdled my milk I will find you, and I will
    kill you.
And at that, my son's hair stood
on end, in the saline.

THE NEW STRANGER

They would peer in the carriage and ask was your father
Chinese, your lustrous, curly-lidded,
slightly tilted eyes, your elegant
forehead. You were a stranger to me –
I thought I would know you, but I had to get to know you –
I knew your bowl brow, and serious
eyes, but sometimes you were alien to me
as a foetus, the large-brained head, the brain
forming its ancient folded flower
like a vegetable, you could not talk,
you looked at me as if from far
away, Mars, the newt, I did not
know you, I had never known a newborn, you
had to arrive into the arms of an amateur.
No one has known my ignorance so well, so
smelled my fear, there, with the fresh
abundant milk. And from no one have I learned
as I learned from you, you brought me forward
from brine and kelp and alkali
through mitosis, meiosis, zygote, delicate
blastocoele, with your eyes I swam up
from deep in your face, with your lips I opened,
with your tongue I formed your name, with the stub of your
hand I budded, with your baby-fat
I put on cells, with your brown, swirling
crown I crowned, with your life I came forth,
and a moment later, rose-blue, you opened
the new package of your breath. I looked
up, and saw you. Hard to tell,
in those first moments on the delivery table,
gore, and cord, and packet of gore,
who has hooked whom – you caught me
into the human. I learned to sit still while you

hauled that whale of milk tail-first down
out of me – split, fiery
flukes of your first sips – I learned to be
nuzzled as they might cuddle an autistic
child. I learned to croon to you,
to cry and moan, and all this time
you were getting your first looks at the earth, it was
you, and I did not know you, I was not
there to greet you, I didn't exist
until you smiled at me, and in your
brilliant loam-colored iris I saw,
tiny as an embryo,
your mother smile.

BACCHANAL IN MEMORY

In the morning, I can hardly remember it,
as if I had not been one of them,
the two so entirely fond of each other,
so loving, and yet not quite all there –
I wish I'd been all there, the blood
so shiny, so opaque, so at random thrown off
the body, by each gesture, I wish I had been
sober for the two or three
alizarin calligraphs on the sheet,
or the lovely trough beside the bath,
herd-pen made of the porcelain tub-wall
and bathmat floor and tile wall, that who-
was-it lowing cunningly in it, that
heifer in it, the milk person,
the blood one, his beloved, his cries
unmusical music. Scrawl tossed off
on the rim of the tub, scarlet sweat
on the wall where the beast in love leaned and wept.
Gore condom in the toilet a moment
like a sea pet in its bowl, the eel
taking our unconceived out to the open ocean –
I liked this couple, I wanted to know them,
they were kind and funny, but there was the language barrier
and the alcohol barrier, and the another planet barrier,
and they did not need me, why would they need me,
there was no longing there, there was matter
realised, as common spirit,
unremembered, no witness left,
precursor of our earth.

AFTER THE RAPE IN OUR BUILDING

The day after we heard about it,
we made love, in the morning, he entered me
and I thought, *It's not so bad*, I could hardly feel anything,
just something hard going in and out of me
somewhere far away down my body
like something seen from a distance, an ocean liner
going down twenty miles away.
It seemed strange I could feel affection for this person
lying on me and doing it,
and yet his hard breasts were dear to me
as if he were under my protection, his whole
skin sweet and rigid with gooseflesh
though I felt nothing. Later, he lay with his
ear against my navel, his long
unshaven cheek on my abdomen as my
guts ground harsh as a young planet
breaking up and re-forming,
and later still he took off the condom, I could not look at him,
he dropped it into an envelope so the kids wouldn't see it,
and dropped the envelope into the wastebasket,
and for the first time, I realised all those
sperm were still alive in there,
skillfully racing around and around in that
ball of dark, white phlegm,
and I could not help it, I thought of the rapist,
of his spirit, that constricted sphere,
sealed and unfruitful.

WHEN IT COMES

Even when you're not afraid you might be pregnant,
it's lovely when it comes, and it's a sexual loveliness,
right along that radiant throat
and lips, the first hem of it,
and at times, the last steps across the bathroom,
you make a dazzling trail, the petals
the flower-girl scatters under the feet of the bride. And then the
    colours of it,
sometimes an almost golden red,
or a black vermilion, the drop that leaps
and opens slowly in the water, gel
sac of a galaxy,
the black-violet, lobed pool, calm
as a lake on the back of the moon, it is all
woundless, even the little spot
in jet and crimson spangled tights who
flings her fine tightrope out
to the left and to the right in that luminous arena,
green upper air of the toilet bowl,
she cannot die. There will be an egg in there,
somewhere, minute, winged with massive
uneven pennons of serum, cell that up
close is a huge, sodden, pocked planet,
but it was not anyone yet. Sometimes,
when I watch the delicate show,
like watching snow, or falling stars,
I think of men, what could it seem to them
that we see the blood pour slowly from our sex,
as if the earth sighed, slightly,
and we felt it, and saw it,
as if life moaned a little, in wonder, and we *were* it.

13

THE FACTORS

Sometimes we seem almost to be working,
as if making something, wrapped tight
around my body from either side as it is
pouring off our gleaming pieces of work, which could be
nearly seen, for a moment, in the air, and we can
hear them, the clear note of their molecular
structure struck –
sometimes you and I are like a factory
minting invisible artifacts,
hot shuddering that floats in air,
more of it is continuously needed,
and more, and more, sometimes we wring
the whole factory like a shimmering rag,
harder each time, the cloth-cries go higher and
higher, from within comes pulsing a lambent
wobbling vessel, off the wheel it
whirls, indented with the muscles' bright thumbs,
transparent with kiln-fire; another is needed,
and another, we don't know who orders it, we are
workers in a doting frenzy of making.
And where is love? This is its room,
where this is done; it is the bed,
the air; and the glowing not-things
wrenched from the body, rushing from it
as though they are being born, those
are acts of love. One could not call it
patience, the hour you kneel, turn,
rise, drawing the, pressing the, made
love out; inside each one
a half-god, calling to the other
half-one, in the other one,
come, come, yes, my darling, my
sweetheart, come.

THE BABYSITTER

The baby was about six months old,
a girl. The length of her life, I had not
touched anyone. That night, when they went out
I held the baby along my arm and
put her mouth to my cotton shirt.
I didn't really know what a person was, I
wanted someone to suck my breast,
I ended up in the locked bathroom,
naked to the waist, holding the baby,
and all she wanted was my glasses, I held her
gently, waiting for her to turn,
like a cherub, and nurse. And she wouldn't, what she wanted
was my glasses. Suck, goddamnit, I thought,
I wanted to feel the tug of another
life, I wanted to feel needed, she grabbed for my
glasses and smiled. I put on my bra
and shirt, and tucked her in, and sang to her
for the last time — clearly it
was the week for another line of work —
and turned out the light. Back in the bathroom,
no light, I lay on the floor, bared
my chest against the icy tiles,
slipped my hand between my legs and
rode, hard, against the kiln-fired floor, my
nipples holding me up off the glazed
aquamarine, as if I were flying,
upside-down, just under the ceiling of the world.

ASPIC AND BUTTERMILK

There were two foods I hated to eat,
so those were foods he liked me to eat.
My father himself could not eat liver – and I could eat liver,
I doted on liver, it was my special meat,
dense and archaic, slightly foul. And he could not eat
rare meat, he fainted at the sight
of a cut – but I could eat *raw* meat,
the velvet of ground-round ground three times,
a spell wound up, the rubble of muscle
in my mouth. But tomato aspic was murky,
it seemed to me like the silt of a wound, he would
watch and see it stay down in me,
as if his exophthalmos eye
held down, on the floor of my stomach, a bolus
stippled with infectus, as I was netted
with his genes. And buttermilk was a joke
on milk, and a joke on butter, my favourites
mingled to make a vomit he wished me to
swallow, while my mother, whose paps I had sucked
and he had probably sucked, watched;
what did it mean, to them, to see
their comminglant pour that sour particulate
refreshment to the back of her throat,
to the liquid jewel of the uvula
and drive it across the sill? A family is a mystery,
the human a mystery – beauty and cruelty,
more passion for life on almost any
terms than death.

BOULDER CREEK

It was time to leave the cabin, the cellar
smelling of apples, the creek in dusk
at noon, the blackberry patch, its thorns
raking the takers of those bite-size nights,
and the pool, small and deep, hand-made
of clay. I don't know where my father
was, probably having one
for the road, with his father, by the fire, in the unlit
room, his mother having one, with them,
alone, in the kitchen, from a jelly glass
with a yellow corn-cob painted on it,
I don't know where my sister was,
but my brother was saying goodbye to the pool,
kneeling at the edge, eighteen months old,
leaning far over, and waving. When
my mother walked by, and looked in the water,
and saw him lying at the bottom, smiling,
she dove in, with her clothes on,
and then there was no one in the air but the clay
ducks, ducks so dry they hissed
when you splashed them, the ducks from church, the ashes
to ashes ducks to ducks ducks. Then the water broke
and she brought him up, dripping goddess
spluttering baby. The drinkers were angry
she had let it happen — while she changed her clothes
they had one for the road. We kept pulling off
the road, for my father to lean out and throw up,
but he would not let her drive until
he almost hit a college boy,
who leaped out of reach, like a doe. The keys exchanged
hands with the noise of the triangles
at school, played underwater or under-
ground. When my father began to snore

in the suicide seat, I curled up in the
niche under the back window,
fit my back to that curve of heavy
post-war glass, and went to sleep,
dreamless. My mother was driving, she was a relative of God's.

ONCE

I saw my father naked, once, I
opened the blue bathroom's door
which he always locked – if it opened, it was empty –
and there, surrounded by glistening turquoise
tile, sitting on the toilet, was my father,
all of him, and all of him
was skin. In an instant, my gaze ran
in a single, swerving, unimpeded
swoop, up: toe, ankle,
knee, hip, rib, nape,
shoulder, elbow, wrist, knuckle,
my father. He looked so unprotected,
so seamless, and shy, like a girl on a toilet,
and even though I knew he was sitting
to shit, there was no shame in that
but even a human peace. He looked up,
I said Sorry, backed out, shut the door
but I'd seen him, my father a shorn lamb,
my father a cloud in the blue sky
of the blue bathroom, my eye had driven
up the hairpin mountain road of the
naked male, I had turned a corner
and found his flank unguarded – gentle
bulge of the hip-joint, border of the pelvic cradle.

Since I was thirteen, I have wondered what I am.
I'd look in the bathroom mirror, stare into that
homely, handsome face — was I nice?
was I evil? — then squeeze, out of my pores,
the slow, thick, cold sebum.
Under my skin, female flesh
lay in packs, hip-flasks of fat.
Out of my mouth came a soil-like smell.
Maybe I was actually dead,
maybe I was my father on the couch passed
out risen up and walking. When I would
touch a boy, I would feel like an archangel
crushed to another archangel,
between the bulge of the dash and the hard
orbit of the seat, wings fiercely shut, we would fly.
I would look in the mirror afterwards, my
eyes shining, was I bad? When the head
appeared, and the child went one way
and my body another, it wasn't good
or evil, it was just the animal,
the real. I sang, while I tended the children,
day and night went back to the sealed
universe of the marriage bed, I felt
virtuous, stuffed to the spirit-tips with touch.
And when the babies grew, I was weaned from them
slowly. I felt I was *nothing* without
someone in my arms, I was a craving spirit,
the way the dead stream along the walls of
houses and affix themselves to the amber windows.
This morning — the rain not dropping, yet, but
fizzing, gently boiling in the air —
I felt some word might be in, soon,
on who I am. And what if I am not loving?

What if all that buttoning, and un-
buttoning, and suckling, and sucking
were the hunger of the dead. Sure I would die for them,
gladly give even my sight, my
hair to flame to save them, but isn't that
easy for the dead, haven't I always really
longed to give an arm for them, to
see the severed arms exchanged on the table.
And sexual love, what if it
is mostly sex, the cunt wanting
to swallow, swallow, fiercely sing all
day all night, what if I'm a selfish
fucker feeding on his pleasure, as if I
could not make
love, when none
had made me. Even her milk she may have craved to
give me to get her poor breast sucked,
and the grave man was finally only
barely able to stay in the suction
path of my beaming. Maybe when I entered
the baby spoon into the mouth, and pulled,
so the sphere of manna stayed in, I was taking,
maybe when I stroke him now, hours
of the night, sated, press my face into the
cool nippleless breast of his buttock, I am
taking. Maybe the pubic hair on the
sheet, by the lamp, this morning, tells it,
rearing up, its shadows' tips
clipped to either end of it,
the twin, under it, running in place
its illusory river – in torque, arched,
the human hair, mated to its shadow,
looks like a soul in hell. I lift my
head and look for you, to give you
this. But what if my giving is taking, if I

set the lips of these words to your breast.
But what if you like that. If we're all takers,
craving to see. So I have set the mouth
of my iris to the mouth of your iris here
for this brief kiss.

TIN

THE WATCHERS

FILM

The car moved slowly, into the frame.
Men were running toward it. In the front seat,
two men, the backs of their necks quite still.
Their hair looked attentive, the tops of their skulls
alert, the scalp itself looked conscious,
as if it had its own brain.
Then men surrounded the car, swarmed it,
mass of sperm mobbing the ovum,
the car afloat in them, stopped – this was
a moment of stillness in the male world.
There was lace in a nearby window, like a net,
there was a shrub, or bush. Then a club appeared,
and someone thudded it, end-first,
against a side window. The men inside
faced forward. *Pound, pound, pound,*
a sound of something being made,
workbench, mallet. Then the quiet crush
of crash-proof glass, then a man turned
and saw the camera, and frowned, and moved
quickly toward us, his hand came up
and grew bigger and bigger, until the screen was dark.

STILL

It is almost a relief to see him again,
to see that they left him his underpants,
hemless, skin-tight, or they have been beaten, slightly,
into his body. They glimmer, a little,
like Jesus' gesso ones, painted on later

25

– and they left him his socks, rolled down to the angle
of the heel. They shot him, they did not beat him
to death, taking him back toward the foetus,
though his hand isn't right, it looks potted, and his naked
flesh is dotted with chips of flesh
and blood and glass and gravel, and here and
there, on him, there is solid dirt –
blackened sock-tips, angle of his elbow
a tuft of earth. Now, the priest
is touching him – when we last saw him, he'd been
waiting for human touch. The twitching
eyelet curtains were thick with eyes –
we stood behind the camera in perfect safety, like demons.

KNOW-NOTHING

Sometimes I think I know nothing about sex.
All that I thought I was going to know,
that I did not know, I still do not know.
I think about this out of town,
on hotel elevators crowded with men.
That body of knowledge which lay somewhere
ahead of me, now I do not know where it
lies, or in the beds of strangers.
I know of sexual love, with my beloved,
but of men – I think there are women who know
men, I can't see what it is
they know, but I feel in myself that I
could know it, or could I have been a woman
who would dare that. I don't mean what she does
with herself, or that she would know more pleasure,
but she knows something true that I don't know,
she knows fucking with a stranger. I feel
in awe of that, why is she not
afraid, what if she did not like
his touch, or what he said, how
would she bear it? Or maybe she has mercy on pretty much
anything a stranger would say or do,
or maybe it is not mercy, but sex,
when she sees what he is like, she enflames for that,
and is afraid of nothing, wanting to touch
stone desire, and know it, she is like
a god, who could have sex with stranger
after stranger – she could know men.
But what of her womb, tender core
of her being, what of her breasts' stiff hearts,
and her dense eggs, what if she falls

in love? Maybe to know sex fully
one has to risk being destroyed by it.
Maybe only ruin could take
its full measure, as death stands
in the balance with birth, and ignorance with love.

THE VISION

We were lying on the bed – and what if we
had just got pregnant? – I have always felt
that I murdered someone, once. When my metal
barrette hit the floor, I said something
scornful about my clumsiness, and you
said, gently, That mean voice you have in-
corporated, it's pretty strong.
And then I felt it: inside me, left side,
vertical, the height of my rib-cage,
someone was standing. My teeth began
to chatter – someone was inside me. It was
a man, lurking. I felt my eyelids
thin in horror; I thought: they have got *inside me*.
They were there in the form of a man hiding
behind a rusted screen door. He was waiting
to kill someone. He was standing calmly,
patient, confident. The place where he stood
was sore as a ten-inch splinter entirely
enclosed. They had got inside me, as a man
on a summer porch, with a woman inside him –
a harpy, entirely enclosed. It was both of them
together, sexual, malicious, eager,
sore. I felt it and felt it, it was in me.
I grabbed my husband's hand and held it
hard to my breastbone, and softly pounded
my breastbone with it. The lurker did not leave
but it dimmed a little. It stands along
my lung. It is waiting to tie someone up.
It is double, it's a couple. All I have to do
is stand here out of range and shout to
anyone who goes near that porch.

THE MAKARIS

Sometimes it seems as if they are trying to get
away from each other, while holding each other
fast, sometimes it looks like torment,
or a grappling with a third thing,
workers wrestling to get something deep into the
ground, they hang on as it hauls them back
and forth, it cannot be seen, though their wetness
glistens on it, they grasp each other
around it, bulging, doubling, maybe they're
creating it, between them, and then,
in her, the pulsings, like birth, like a beloved
crowning. She rests, and then more harrowing
joy-work, like a newborn's large shoulders. She rests,
then the arms, the jointed gasps, she rests, then the
waist, through this waist of her body, which, convulsing,
indents it, for a moment the two hourglasses
gleam, aligned. She rests, then the next,
like a sex, birthed, she rests, then the last
wrenchings, the long lathe-turning of a thigh,
knee, calf, ow, ow,
ankle, arch, I love you, I love you,
toe-tip, air –
the outline judders between them, and then
he fiercely fills it, full, she holds them,
there are tears on all their faces, he casts himself
into it, he gives it his heart.
And then they rest, in unison,
flesh, and luminous something, and flesh,
it fits between them, it is the light
which is joining them, they have made it, it quivers,
a being as if from another place,
like an almost-lost species, and if they are false
to each other, it is the one they murder.

THE NECKLACE

At the worst of the depression, one moment in the office,
suddenly, my necklace shifted,
flowed across some high ribs
and sank down along the top of one breast
as if a creature had got into my shirt,
yet I felt its will-lessness, caress
of matter only, small whipper or
snapper, milk or garter, just
the vertebrae now, as if a stripped
spine had taken its coccyx in its jaw
around my throat's equator, and now
stirred on the mortal plates. And these were
the pearls from my mother, as if she slithered
along me to say, Come away from your gloom,
your father, that garden is a grave, come away,
come away — as if some crumbs of her milquetoast,
aged and polished to a gem hardness,
spoke in oyster Braille on my chest
near my own breast, suckler singing
to suckler, anti-Circe my mother
led me away from that trough with a light
raking, over me, of her wiggly whip — just one
wobble along me, globe on her axis,
chariot-wheel of morning.

DEAR HEART,

How did you know to turn me over,
then, when I couldn't know to take
the moment to turn and start to begin
to finish, I was out there, far ahead
of my body, far ahead of the earth,
ahead of the moon – like someone on the other
side of the moon, stepped off, facing space, I was
floating out there, splayed, facing
away, fucked, fucked, my face,
glistening and distorted, pressed against the inner
caul of the world. I was almost beyond
pleasure, in a region of icy, absolute
sensing, my open mouth and love-slimed
cheeks stretching the membrane the way
the face of the almost born can appear, still
veiled in its casing, just inside
the oval portal, pausing, about
to split its glistering mask – you eased me
back, drew me back into the human
night, you turned me and the howling slowed, and at the
crux of our joining, flower-heads grew
fast-motion against you, swelled and burst without
tearing – ruinless death, each
sepal, each petal, came to the naught
of earth, our portion, in ecstasy, ash
to fire to ash, dust to bloom to dust.

THE ELOPEMENT

It was raining upwards, sideways, each
tree bursting with rain like brilliant
sweat. We stopped at a country store
to ask where we could get married. There were vats
of pickles, barrels of square yellow crackers,
the Prop. gave us the local J. P.'s
number. It was gently misting, in there,
brine and cracker-salt. The J. P. asked
if we'd get married in his church. While he called his minister
I wandered, in the dark, store
air, past the columns of vertebrate tin.
The shelves, and floor, and counters were old
wood, there must have been mice in the building,
rats, a cat, roaches, beetles,
and, in the barrel, whatever makes water
pickle, the mother of vinegar, it was
a spore Eden, a bestiary,
the minister said Yes, come right on over,
but maybe we had been married, there,
by matter, by the pickles, by the crackers, by the balls
of guard-fur, the rats looking away
into the long reaches, like the cows
in the manger, by the crèche, though there's always one
who widens her glowing eyes, and gazes – one
rat, transfixed by mortal coupling
grabbed the Dutch Girl cocoa tin in his
arms and spun her in a dervish mazurka,
then all the witnesses waltzed, the Campbell's-soup
twins, the Gerber baby, Aunt
Jemima, Betty Crocker, the Sun Maid
raisin girl, the oats Quaker,
the chef of Cream of Wheat, every
good, mild, family guest

danced at our marriage, cloudy ions in the
cucumber-barrel spiraled, our eggs and
sperm swam, in tandem, in water-
ballet, the spores of the sky whirled and
kissed on our wedding day.

When we took the acid, his wife was off
with someone else, there was a hole in their bedroom
wall where the Steuben wedding owl
had flown from one room right into another,
I was in love with his best friend, who had
gone into a monastery
after he'd deflowered me, so we
knew each other – when he finished, under
my palm I could feel the circular ribs of his
penis, I finished, with my legs wrapped around his
leg, even with my toes pointed, my
feet reached only halfway down
his calf, later I was lying on the bathroom
floor, looking up at him, naked, he was
6′6″, a decathlete,
my eyes followed the inner line of his
leg, up, up, up,
up, up, up, up.
Weeks later, he would pull a wall-phone
out of a wall, and part of the wall, he would
cross the divider in his Mustang with me and go
60, against 2 a.m. traffic, crying, I could
hardly hear what he said about the barbed
wire and his father and his balls – but that
acid night, we stayed up all night, I was
not in love with him, so his beauty made me
happy, we chattered, we chatted naked, he
told me everything he liked
about my body – and he liked everything –
even the tiny gooseflesh bumps
around my hard nipples,
he said the way to make love to me
would be from behind, with that sheer angle, his

forefinger drew it, gently, the deep
hair-pin curve of the skinny buttocks,
he said it the way I thought an older
cousin in a dream might give advice
to a younger cousin, his fingertip
barely missing my – whatever, in love, one would
call the asshole, he regarded me with a
savouring kindness, from some cleft of sweetness in the
human he actually looked at me
and thought how I best should be fucked. *Oooh.*
Oooh . . . It meant there was something to be done with me,
something exactly right, he looked at me
and saw it,
willing to not be the one
who did it – all night, he desired me and
protected me, he gazed at my body and un-
saw my parents' loathing, pore by
pore on my skin he closed that old couple's eyes.

THE SEEKER

Suddenly, at night, in a strange town,
in somebody's borrowed car, VW
smelling of a man I have not met,
suede, cords, smoke, emotion,
I remember the thrill of the strangeness of a man,
the newness of a new mouth, not
knowing the arc of the teeth, wild
model on the dentist's shelf, not
recognizing the satin of the gum,
necking too soon with a man in his car,
setting the curves of my sweater to his palms,
not knowing him well enough
to guess if he is dangerous,
putting the tasting first, the unknown
tongue, scoring cheek, pattern
of the bristles, like a toy bed of nails,
a test of faith, an intricate coal
drawn across my skin – the other,
the one who seemed to come from almost out-
side the human, as in my imagined
conception my father had come up to me,
somewhere, I was not a creature, just salt
and oil, and he moved close, and with something like
a deep kiss brought me into existence.
Sometimes, when I necked with a stranger, I went
close to that – pheromone, sweat,
scorch, kiss of life – tasting in him
some male, unmothered world, and through him
a male world was tasting me.
Every time, I was pretending, without knowing,
that I could lay my body like a soul in his hands
and he would not take it. But he might. But he would not.

THE DAY THEY TIED ME UP

None of the pain was sharp. The sash
was soft, its cotton blunt, like a bandage
it held my wrist to the chairs. And the fierce
glazed string of the woven seat
printed me in deep pink, but I was
used to that, that matter could mark us
and its marks dissolve. That day, no one touched me,
it was a formal day, the nerves lay easy
in their planched grooves. The hunger grew, but
quietly, edgeless, a suckling in my stomach
doubling, it was a calm day
unfolding to its laws. Only the pleasure had been
sharp – the tilt of the squat bottle
over their bed, the way the ink
lowered itself, onto the spread, I had
felt its midnight, genie shape
leave my chest, pouring forth, and it was
India ink, the kind that does not come out,
I sat attached to the chair like Daphne
halfway out of the wood, and I read that blot.
I read it all day, like a Nancy Drew I was
in – they had said *You won't be fed
till you say you're sorry*, I was strangely happy, I would
never say I was sorry, I had left
that life behind. So it didn't surprise me when she
came in slowly, holding a bowl that
held what swayed and steamed, she sat and
spoon-fed me, in silence, hot
alphabet soup. Sharp pleasure
of my wing-tip hands hanging down beside me
slack as I ate, sharp pleasure of the
little school of edible letters flowing
in, over my taste-buds, B,

O, F, K, G,
I mashed the crescent moon of the C,
caressed the E, reading with my tongue
that boiled Braille – and she was almost kneeling to me
and I wasn't sorry. She was feeding the one
who wasn't sorry, the way you lay food
at the foot of an image. I sat there, tied,
taking in her offering
and wildly reading as I ate, S S F
T, L W B B P Q
B, she dipped into my mouth the mild
discordant fuel – she wanted me to thrive, and decipher.

TAKE THE I OUT

But I love the I, steel I-beam
that my father sold. They poured the pig iron
into the mold, and it fed out slowly,
a bending jelly in the bath, and it hardened,
Bessemer, blister, crucible, alloy, and he
marketed it, and bought bourbon, and Cream
of Wheat, its curl of butter right
in the middle of its forehead, he paid for our dresses
with his metal sweat, sweet in the morning
and sour in the evening. I love the *I*,
frail between its flitches, its hard ground
and hard sky, it soars between them
like the soul that rushes, back and forth,
between the mother and father. What if they had loved each other,
how would it have felt to be the strut
joining the floor and roof of the truss?
I have seen, on his shirt-cardboard, years
in her desk, the night they made me, the penciled
slope of her temperature rising, and on
the peak of the hill, first soldier to reach
the crest, the Roman numeral I –
I, I, I, I,
girders of identity, head on,
embedded in the poem. I love the *I*
for its premise of existence – our I – when I was
born, part gelid, I lay with you
on the cooling table, we were all there, a
forest of felled iron. The *I* is a pine,
resinous, flammable root to crown,
which throws its cones as far as it can in a fire.

AFTER PUNISHMENT WAS DONE WITH ME

After punishment was done with me,
after I would put my clothes back on,
my mother's hairbrush scansion done,
I'd go back to my room, close the door,
and wander around, ending up
on the floor sometimes, always, near the baseboard,
where the vertical fall of the wall meets
the level rule of the floor – I would put
my face near that angle, and look at the dust
and anything caught in the dust. I would see
the wedding swags of old-lady-hair –
pelmets carved on cenotaph granite –
and cocoons of slough like tiny Kotexes
wound and wound in toilet paper,
I would see the anonymous crowds of grit, as if
looking down into Piazza Navona
from a mile above Il Duce, I would see
a larval casing waisted in gold
thin as the poorest gold wedding band,
and a wasp's dried thorax and legs wound love-ring
with a pubic hair of my mother's. I would see
the coral-maroon of the ladybug's back
marked with its two, night genes,
I would see a fly curled up, dried,
its wings like the rabbit's ears, or the deer's.
I would lie quiet and look at them,
it was so peaceful there with them,
I was not at all afraid of them,
and my sadness for them didn't matter.
I would look at each piece of lint
and half imagine being it,
I would feel that I was looking at
the universe from a great distance.

Sometimes I'd pick up a Dresden fly
and gaze at it closely, sometimes I'd idly play
house with the little world, weddings and
funerals with barbed body parts,
awful births, but I did not want
to disarrange that unerring deadness
like a kind of goodness, corner of wetless
grey waste, nothing the human
would go for. Without desire or rage
I would watch that atom celestium as the pain
on my matter died and turned to spirit
and wandered the cloud world of home,
the ashes of the earth.

IMMERSION COIL

Its curled forelock goes into the water
in the cup in the hotel room, its plug into the wall.
No life, yet, no murmur on the planet,
then after a moment
a hank of water
kinks, and torques into a murk of kink
blur, as if my father un-died,
sat up. I have thought that a woman's desire was the
strongest thing on earth, I have not seen
that they crave us as much as we crave them. Go back before
my father's indifference, he sits on the lawn,
in summer, in his bathing suit, his shapely
legs naked, their hairs wavy
and evenly placed, like the undersurface
of the topsoil's tapestry, the root-hairs of heaven,
a two-year-old girl runs into the V
of his open legs, and out again, her
nape-quirks jump, and the ruffles of her rhumba-seat
playsuit ripple, she runs back in,
and he sends her out, he watches the wave-lengths of
hair and ribbon writhe on this female
flesh of his flesh, he will tell the story
until he dies, rolling his Eden-ploughed-
under eyes.

WHAT IS THE EARTH?

The earth is a homeless person. Or
the earth's home is the atmosphere.
Or the atmosphere is the earth's clothing,
layers of it, the earth wears all of it,
the earth is a homeless person.
Or the atmosphere is the earth's cocoon,
which it spun itself, the earth is a larvum.
Or the atmosphere is the earth's skin –
earth, and atmosphere, one
homeless one. Or its orbit is the earth's
home, or the path of the orbit just
a path, the earth a homeless person.
Or the gutter of the earth's orbit is a circle
of hell, the circle of the homeless. But the earth
has a place, around the fire, the hearth
of our star, the earth is at home, the earth
is home to the homeless. For food, and warmth,
and shelter, and health, they have earth and fire
and air and water, for home they have
the elements they are made of, as if
each homeless one were an earth, made
of milk and grain, like Ceres, and one
could eat oneself – as if the human
were a god, who could eat the earth, a god
of homelessness.

STRAW

A VISION

Suddenly, staring at a motel wall,
I saw it – my husband's honour. It was
a flower, dark-cream, the petals curved
like limbs, he was holding it, I looked
again, and it was a tiny newborn,
the baby of our faithfulness.
It moved, a little, in his hands, a spirit
in human hands. I feel that I
would die for it, as if it were like
our daughter and son. No one has come back
to tell us how it feels to die
saving your child, knowing your child
will live – tasting, in your mouthful of blood,
your child's long life. To call it a pleasure
to die for love . . . I looked at his honour
more closely, perhaps it was not a baby
or blossom he held, moving luminous
bouquet, but the human genitals,
the pair together, clasped swallowtails
over the garden. He stood there floating them
above his palms, they were coming, grave
brilliant wrenches mid-air, and when there was
only one being there
I saw it was the soul.

THE SOUND

The morning our daughter has come home, I hear
a sound, over my head – like angels,
or the pinging in my ears, sometimes,
in bed, or the noise of a planet's ring,
the whir of dry grit around it.
It comes and goes, a cosmic zinging,
finally I realise it's a woman singing,
actually, a woman humming
in the room above me – it's our girl, unpacking –
the floorboards creak, I hear it and then don't,
as if a wind carries it unevenly,
clear, high, casual, watery humming.
It sounds like a summer band at a distance,
or music made with the back of the mind,
purposeless, melodious chaff of a
woman puttering, her soprano saying
Here is no harm, we improvise
on the edge of milk and sleep. And it's
so intimate, without witness,
as if I were hearing the workings of her muscles
as she lifts and unfolds, each garment doubles,
quadruples like the zygote. I have never, before, heard a
grown woman singing alone –
my mother mostly yoo-hooed to a male
God, gorgeously screamed for help –
now, below our daughter's crooning,
I lean, here, like a newborn freshly
arrived in a home, or an embryo
in the belly of a woman whom homecoming has made
musical, the body's harmony
audible, as if matter itself were merciful.

Starfish rubble and sand on the floor
of the community centre – '50s music,
the kids had stayed home, so we could shimmy without
them rolling their eyes. Inside me, Meursault,
and love's little swimmers, still flashing up
into the deeper dark inside me,
we had gone through Aretha, Elvis, Fats,
Platters, Pretenders, we had worked out,
our shirts stuck to our chests and backs, it was a
slow dance, we were plastered together *In the*
Still (Sho Dotin' Shoby Doe)
of the Nii, ii, ii, iight, I could
smell a wreath of smells of our bodies
rising around us, your hands a large
knot at the small of my back, my arms
up around your neck, crook of my
elbow hooking your nape, I thought of my
self, fourteen, walleyed flower of the
junior-high dance, grain of the pine
printing my spine as I watched Kit Gibbs and his
stacked blonde
slow dance
thirty years ago, my cheek
pressed the salt grit of your jaw my
length your length, I could hardly believe it,
till death do us part, I said to myself,
till death do us part.

OUTDOOR SHOWER

Crusted with dried brack, dusted with
sand, shaking from the cold Atlantic,
hair gristled with crystals, tangled with the
jellied palps of wrack – just step on this
slatted rack, pull the iron
handle of the forged world toward you.
The sluice courses, down your shin,
in a swirling motion, milk smoke, the
silky rush of fresh water, supple and alkaline.
Lids clenched, you reach for the small
oil torso of soap, run it
along your limbs and whirl it over the points of the
three-point shower star of sex:
arm-pit, arm-pit, sex. Then the gritty
dial of your face, lather it, bring it
under the coursing, and open your mouth,
stone-sweet well-water,
and then the head,
delve it in so the sand around the scalp
dances like the ions at the edges of matter,
and the shampoo, mild soldier,
take her by the shoulders and pour the pale eel on your head. Then
    feel them going:
salp, chitin, diatom, dulse, the
blind ones of the ocean. Rinse until
it pours down your head like water, the dark
descendant pelf of the land. Now open your eyes –
green lawn, silver pond,
grey dune, blue Atlantic,
the simple fields of God, liquid and solid.
Turn and turn in hot water,

column of heat in the cool wind
and sunny air, squeeze your eyes and then
open them again – look, it is still there,
the world as heaven, your body at the edge of it.

THE REMEDY

He did not have a fever, but he looked
rumpled, and blurred, sitting up in bed,
in a worn T-shirt, and reading glasses,
his throat sore, though he still looked buoyant
and sated from last night.
As I walked toward the kitchen, I felt strangely calm,
as if I had lived for a long time.
At first, the jar would not open, my hands felt as
weak as my knees – then, the grainy,
slow, give. I took our gentlest
table knife, one we have had
for twenty-five years, I turned its tip in the
white ochre of the whipped honey and with
care unfurled a jot of it
on one hard nipple, and then the other. It looked
right, to me, the tips of the teats
clothed, the cloth woven by the bee,
an offering, a gold weave
laid at the breast, glistening
on this flesh – where milk was, honey shall be,
where the small mouths had drawn, the grown
mouth will rove, bringing my soul forward with a cry
then both our souls forward with birth-room crying.

LEAVING THE ISLAND

On the ferry, on the last morning of summer,
a father at the snack counter deep in the boat
gets breakfast for the others. *Here, let me drink some of*
Mom's coffee, so it won't be so full
for you to carry, he says to his son,
a boy of ten or eleven. The boat
lies lower and lower in the water as the last
cars drive on, it tilts its massive
grey floor like the flat world. Then the
screaming starts, *I carry four things,*
and I only give you one, and you drop it,
what are you, a baby? a high, male
shrieking, and it doesn't stop, *Are you two?*
Are you a baby? I give you one thing,
no one in the room seems to move for a second,
a steaming pool spreading on the floor, little
sea with its own waves, the boy
at the shore of it. *Can't you do anything*
right? Are you two? Are you two?, the piercing
cry of the father. *Go away,*
go up to your mother, get out of here –
the purser swabbing the floor, the boy
not moving from where the first word touched him,
and I could not quite walk past him, I paused
and said I *spilled my coffee on the deck, last trip,*
it happens to us all. He turned to me,
his lips averted so the gums gleamed,
he hissed a guttural hiss, and in
a voice like Gollum's or the Exorcist girl's when she
made that stream of vomit and beamed it
eight feet straight into the minister's mouth

he said *Shut up, shut up, shut up*, as if
protecting his father, peeling from himself
a thin wing of hate, and wrapping it
tightly around father and son, shielding them.

AT HOME

Then, when he is drifting off,
at home in nearly empty space,
almost as if at home near death,
it is a comfort to faintly stroke his eyelid,
maybe the closest there is, on him,
to a cervix, and to lay my face
in his palm, in his sleep, gum its heel
like a newborn hunter, take his longest
finger down my throat to touch
the uvula, who loves to let him
touch her, drop at the end of that drip
of nectar. I do not want to leave his face,
I have just, about, over and over,
entered it, my eyes in his head
and his in mine, my mouth in his mouth,
with licks and kisses I miss where I have nearly
been, my brain in his brain – we have held
skulls like hands, now he's sleeping a little,
point of honour not to wake him,
point of pleasure to wake him perhaps
once, the portcullis lifts, and he seems to not
know what he is seeing, for a moment sleeping
with his eye open – it is visible, the pure
spirit of the spiritless rods
and cones, then his sight rolls up, sea moon
up into cloud-bank. He naps, but I do not
want to let him go, I feel
delicious, remembering desire, the ways
he increased and increased it. His eyelid lifts –
justice, mercy. We look at each other
till our eyes are wet, then we rest awhile,
and then we stare at each other, almost
emotionless with sex and trust.

I take his silky hair gently in my
fist and squeeze it, as if his scalp
speaks. I graze his crow's-feet with my thumbs,
like a child learning to use both hands
at once. Our groans, and soft laughs,
of the last hours, lie everywhere
in the room, on every surface.

THE BED

My father's new wife was looking out a window
in their first apartment, hands in the suds,
when she saw a tall, dark-haired teenager
turn the corner. That's his girl,
she said to herself. She had never seen me,
she looked at me, and knew me. In a minute
the bell rang, and there I stood
on his long legs, under the stook of
his dark hair. I gazed at her –
this was the woman my father loved.
My father was in love! She fed me something,
I ate and beheld until we heard his key
in the lock. Surprise! Surprise! He saw us
standing together, flushed, blushing –
in the heat of the moment, softened metals,
we three were joined. Years later,
when we stood on either side of him
and he sank away, our bond would not break,
the way the last child in crack-the-whip
may fly, feet off the ground, and the chain
hold. That day, we stood together,
cheeks hot, then my father led us
over to a wall with three grooves in it
like the cut outline of a doorway, he pushed
a button – and down, out of the wall, fell
a double bed, its legs bounced
on the floor, it danced while he laughed. Their Murphy
bed of love! In the night, he said, it would
close, suddenly, like a book slamming, they would
wake up upright smashed against the wall, we
beamed at each other. After that,
when I thought of them, I thought of their bed
snapping shut, like a mouse trap,

holding them pressed there, against the wall,
in violent climax, crushed together,
flowers in a book, so flat they're transparent,
the stamen indented into the pistil,
the anther bent over the petal, the man
and woman as God had made them, almost
my parents, in love.

MY MOTHER'S PANSIES

And all that time, in back of the house,
there were pansies growing, some silt blue,
some silt yellow, most of them sable
red or purplish sable, heavy
as velvet curtains, so soft they seemed wet but they were
dry as powder on a luna's wing,
dust on an alluvial path, in a drought
summer. And they were open like lips,
and pouted like lips, and had a tiny fur-gold
v, which made bees not be able
to not want. And so, although women, in our
lobes and sepals, our corollas and spurs, seemed
despised spathe, style-arm, standard,
crest, and fall,
still there were those plush entries,
night mouth, pillow mouth,
anyone might want to push
their pinky, or anything, into such velveteen
chambers, such throats, each midnight-velvet
petal saying touch-touch-touch, please-touch, please-touch,
each sex like a spirit – shy, flushed, praying.

THE PREPOSITIONS

When I started Junior High, I thought
I'd probably be a Behaviour Problem
all my life, John Muir Grammar
the spawning grounds, the bad-seed bed, but
the first morning at Willard, the dawn
of seventh grade, they handed me a list
of forty-five prepositions, to learn
by heart. I stood in the central courtyard,
enclosed garden that grew cement,
my pupils followed the line of the arches
up and over, up and over, like
alpha waves, *about, above,*
across, along, among, around, an
odd comfort began, in me,
before, behind, below, beneath,
beside, between, I stood in that sandstone
square, and started to tame. *Down,*
from, in, into, near, I was
located there, watching the Moorish half-
circles rise and fall. *Off,*
on, onto, out, outside, we
came from sixth grades all over the city
to meet each other for the first time,
White tennis-club boys who did not
speak to me, White dorks
who did, Black student-council guys who'd gaze
off, above my head, and the Black
plump goof-off, who walked past and
suddenly flicked my sweater-front, I thought to shame me.
Over, past, since, through,
that was the year my father came home in the
middle of the night with those thick earthworms
of blood on his face, trilobites of

60

elegant gore, cornice and crisp
waist of the extinct form,
till, to, toward, under, the
lining of my uterus convoluted,
shapely and scarlet as the jointed leeches
of wound clinging to my father's face in that
mask, *unlike, until, up,* I'd
walk, day and night, into
the Eden of the list, *hortus enclosus* where
everything had a place. I was *in
relation to, upon, with,* and when I
got to forty-five I could start over,
pull the hood of the list down over
my brain again. It was the first rest
I had had from my mind. My glance would run
slowly along the calm electro-
cardiogram of adobe cloister,
within, without, I'd repeat the prayer I'd
received, a place in the universe,
meaningless but a place, an exact location –
Telegraph, Woolsey, Colby, Russell –
Berkeley, 1956,
fourteen, the breaking of childhood, beginning of memory.

If, when you first arrived, I looked
down, and saw you as lines of spore
chevroning out in a dish, if I saw you
as cracks appearing in the groin's double crystal,
showing the night inside, if I saw you
as strands flung out, from the mid-line of my naked
pubis, by the orb-spider
of sex and death, if I saw you as a small
mass of threads on the sewing floor,
detritus of the chopped pattern
and the hem, dust-ball of snips, if I saw you as
waste on the children's barbershop floor, a
rough bouquet of lockets, a puff-ball of
shorn, a bright tumbleweed,
if, when I first saw you, I saw you
as soft, iron filings, lining
up, diagonal, at either side,
as if magnetised, if I saw you as fine
lines of excremental seepage
appearing there, your brushwork blurring
the angles – oh down on the wings, print
rising from the open book, shade's
steam, forgive me, you are the loveliest
shyest frond of fern, herb
of elixir – beloved, you are Elysium, not
the earth we emerge from and enter, but the garden
just above the earth, its heaven.

THE TRY-OUTS

'*Rat!* Torturing my *BRAIN!*' is the aria
my mother sang, trying out to be a singer
in a downtown theatre. All month, she had practiced,
'*Rat!*' leaping out in sharp coloratura
from that mouth that drew back from kissing my father,
her mouth I kissed as if it were sacred,
'*Rat!*' suddenly in the pantry, then the pause, then
torturing and *my* run together in a
slurred mutter, then that radical, stridulating
high, off-key note, '*BRAIN!*'
– this was how a woman tried
to enter the world, *Rat torturing my*
brain vacuuming, *rat torturing my*
brain doing the dishes, atonal
shriek like choir gone wrong, or as if
the housework, itself, screamed, matter
and dirt-on-matter squealing, the dust-rings of
Saturn grating on each other. Backstage,
the folds of a massive curtain, and the mothers were
going behind its lank volutes,
one by one, and trying out,
Rat torturing my brain, I could tell
my mother by her pitch, about an eighth of an
inch below the note, and by
the way my skin tightened, and rose, and I
cried, when she sang. I would stop making
the paper Easter basket, and shudder
till another mother sang. At least I thought they were all mothers,
those grown-up women, although I was the only
child, there, cutting strips of
construction paper in the bad light
down at the base of the blackout aurora,
cloak of a potentate, where you wait

to be born, where your mother prays to be famous.
I never wondered just how the rat
tortured her brain, I cut out bunnies and
chickens and stood them up inside a basket
by bending them hard at the ankles, and taping
their feet to the floor. My jaws moved
with the scissors, chewing – it was a sort
of eating, that making, a having by pouring
forth, hearing from the dark the soprano
off-key cries of my kind.

MY FATHER'S DIARY

When I sit on the bed, and spring the brass
scarab legs of its locks, inside
is the stacked, shy wealth of his print.
He could not write in script, so the pages
are sturdy with the beamwork of printedness,
WENT TO LOOK AT A CAR, DAD IN A
GOOD MOOD AT DINNER, LUNCH WITH MOM,
TRIED OUT SOME RACQUETS – a life of ease,
except when he spun his father's DeSoto on the
ice, and a young tree whirled up
to the hood, throwing up her arms – until
LOIS. PLAYED TENNIS WITH LOIS, LUNCH
WITH MOM AND LOIS, DRIVING WITH LOIS,
LONG DRIVE WITH LOIS. And then,
LOIS! I CAN'T BELIEVE IT! SHE IS SO
GOOD, SO SWEET, SO GENEROUS, I HAVE
NEVER, WHAT HAVE I EVER DONE
TO DESERVE SUCH A GIRL? Between the tines
of his Ws, and liquid on the serifs, moonlight,
the self of the grown boy pouring
out, kneeling in pine-needle weave,
worshipping her. It was my father
good, it was my father grateful,
it was my father dead, who had left me
these small structures of his young brain –
he wanted me to know him, he wanted
someone to know him.

BY EARTH

I will lie at the front of a church, in a box,
a kind of low, dirt altar,
I will be inside it, on my back, without
breath, without brain, and my friends
will come by, they will be only the grain
of the wood away, its pouring water,
someone might lay a palm on it, as if
resting a hand on a waterfall.
They will not hate me for being mortal.
They will know I can't help it – the frenum, grimace, stroke-
flung-down hands. They'll forgive the blood
congealed, the shit bacterium
passing, at last, through the walls, into
the whole body. I used to want to
ask my mother to forgive me for my life,
for my body that stood in the light of her death,
and for my rogue mind – she wanted a boy
obedient to her, I came here without
a penis, and judged her. She could not forgive
my two, non-blue eyes, one
the soil-black pansy, one the loam-brown
Mourning Cloak. And later, when hair
poured from my cruxes, like a corpse's in the grave,
I felt as if she did not like it,
she did not want more matter of his matter,
or even of her own. But my friends will forgive
my bark hide, the deadwood of my bones,
the gloss of my mound of Venus could be like a
hill grove in their mind while I rot, they will forgive my rot,
the microbes flooding through me like silt over
an ocean floor. Even my nipples
will die, these hard hearts that I count on,

I will lie in my coffin easy as a baby
asleep at the center of a family – I love
your life-line, I love your love-line, I love them on the
rosewood roof of my heaven, the balsam cot.

FIRE

BY FIRE

When I pass an abandoned, half-wrecked building,
on a waste-lot, in winter, the smell of the cold
rot decides me – I am not going
to rot. I will not lie down in the ground
with the cauliflower and the eggshell mushroom,
and grow a fungus out of my stomach
steady as a foetus, my face sluicing off me,
my Calvinist lips blooming little
broccolis, my hair growing,
my nails growing into curls of horn, so there is
always movement in my grave. If the worm
were God, let it lope, slowly, through my flesh, if its
loping were music. But I was near, when ferment
moved, in its swerving tunnels, through my father,
nightly, I have had it with that,
I am going to burn, I am going to pour my
body out as fire, as fierce
pain not felt I am leaving. The hair
will fizzle around my roasting scalp, with a
head of garlic in my pocket I am going out.
And I know what happens in the fire closet,
when the elbow tendons shrink in the heat, and I
want it to happen – I want, dead, to
pull up my hands in fists, I want
to go out as a pugilist.

WARRIOR: 5TH GRADE

I don't remember who had set it up,
but I knew, all day, that when night came,
at the sleepover, at Dinny Craviotto's,
I would challenge Shelly Ashby to a fight
for picking on Betty Jean Hadden. I knew
public opinion was behind me, my mouth and
fists and lungs were swollen, slightly,
with nobleness. All day I was modest,
eyes cast down in righteousness, I was
the scourge of the John Muir Brownie Troop, I was a
moral instrument. I was very happy,
that night I would get to hit someone.
I had had a couple of fights, before,
and I loved the slight give of the body, the
contraption of the fist, like a small dollhouse
filled with erasers and rocks, and the free
swing through the air, that sideways plummet,
and the hit, the crunching noise, the rubbery
curve of the ribs, their spring, I wanted
to hurt someone, someone bad,
and be hurt, I wanted to be hit when I
could hit back. I wasn't thinking of
my mother's blows, which anyway weren't
flesh on flesh, she kept the taken
tortoise carapace between us, but she
swung with passion, I wanted to be
like her, and hit, and hit, and hit.
I had my style decided on –
left arm whirling, David's sling,
my fist its stone, right arm jabbing
out and back, fast, I was a
threshing-machine of punishment, I would
move across the Craviotto living-room un-

beatable, I would harvest Shelly Ashby,
bitter Brownie with the pouting bee-bit lips.
And I don't remember what came next, I remember
a circle of faces, an outer circle
of trussed-up sleeping-bags, lumps,
camels kneeling in the desert, I remember
nothing about it for years, until
it came to me that I thought that my lover was too
gentle – I was twenty – I realised that I wanted to be
fucked blind, pummelled half dead with it.

FIRE ESCAPE

It held with rusted struts to the rear
corner of the wedding-cake hotel,
and it was made of rust, five-storey spiral
cylinder. We would loiter near it,
then stumble through the studded door. Slammed, it would
echo with the clang of a metal keel,
and it must have been made in a foundry, laid on its
side while the helix was rivetted into it,
or else the curly chute had been created
first, enormous ship's screw,
the casing soldered around it. Oxidising
upright, long abandoned, it stood among
eucalyptus, when we slipped into its base it was
lightless, by feel we climbed the steep
corkscrew, jamming our palms and soles
against the wall and central pole,
and the first one up would hide on the shallow
sill of a blocked exit, and quietly
scream – smell of iron lichen,
grit of spiculate, falling gravel,
darkness a cushion against your face.
At the top, the ramp stopped – just stopped,
cut off, two feet below the roof's lid,
it was one of the points of doing it
to go up to the top, and dangle over
at your waist, into nothing. And then the descent –
sit, hold to the lip of the slant, and let
go, plummet in the whirling clockwise
rush of water when you pull the plug,
I would drop down through it, silent, illegal,
unseeing, heart half-stopped, a globule
of matter, a sperm in my father, who is not even
horizontal, now – burned up, ash.

When the witch flew up to the left right left I
remembered it – wasn't there something
sharp which had soared into the sky on a spiral like
that over Jerusalem? The only other
movie I had seen, every Good Friday,
was the Crucifixion documentary,
noon to three, and wasn't this
the cloud-cover, from over the crosses,
their delicate shapes thickened and distorted,
stuck with their grievous human gum,
above them the liquid dart of the witch
streaked. And wasn't the witch's home,
near Oz, Golgotha? Her broom had been the stick
on which they had stuck the vinegar sop, I
recognised it, the same prop, and the
field of poppies, wasn't that
Gethsemane? And the witch wanted
to torture them to death, like Jesus
– blood, tin, straw – what they
were made of was to be used to kill them.
And she lived on a hill, like Calvary, where the
crosses stuck out like pins from the globe – or
would it have been worse in a pit, look down
and see the crosses set up below us
in the scooped-out fruit of the earth. And parts
of the castle looked Roman, as if Dorothy
were back in the underpopulated time, the
eerie empty world. But what *was*
that harsh projectile scrap of cinder which
pulled across the screen, turned, reversed,
and was sucked up? Nothing went up, that
day, off the tussock of execution,
they brought him down, to the ground, down

the hill, laid him down, in the tomb
– and yet, when the Wicked Witch of the West soared
up, it was over the Crucifixion, there
must have been a piece of fluff on the
film or a disc of soot pointed like a
burnt thing, caught in an updraft.
I remember when Jesus died the trees
bent and groaned, there was a strong wind, we were murderers.

Then dirt scared me, because of the dirt
he had put on her face. And her training bra
scared me – the newspapers, morning and evening,
kept saying it, *training bra*,
as if the cups of it had been calling
the breasts up, he buried her in it,
perhaps he had never bothered to take it
off, and they had found her underpants
in a garbage can. And I feared the word
eczema, like my acne and like
the X in the paper which marked her body,
as if he had killed her for not being flawless.
I feared his name, Burton Abbott,
the first name that was a last name,
as if he was not someone specific.
It was nothing one could learn from his face.
His face was dull and ordinary,
it took away what I'd thought I could count on
about evil. He looked thin, and lonely,
it was horrifying, he looked almost humble.
I felt awe that dirt was so impersonal,
and pity for the training bra,
pity and terror of eczema.
And I could not sit on my mother's electric
blanket anymore, I began to have
a fear of electricity –
the good people, the parents, were going
to fry him to death. This was what
his parents had been telling us:
Burton Abbott, Burton Abbott,
death to the person, death to the home planet.

The worst thing would have been to think
of her, of what it had been to be her,
alive, to be walked, alive, into that cabin,
to look into those eyes, and see the human.

THE BURNED DIARY

She lay down, in her world, in its concentric
layers, her diary one leaf of the nutmeat,
her family around her in pinion folds, she
slept, and the evicted tenants poured fuel
on the walls of the apartment under her,
head of the match like the char ball of
terra in an aureole of burning hair, she
breathed in the smoke as if it were air.
She never knew her parents as a couple
parted – bride of her father in his long
white, baker apron, sunk beside
a shut door, groom of her mother
charred on the kitchen floor, or the super
on the roof, above her window, shouting
down like a seraphim, or the cop climbing halfway
to her, through hell. And when the dawn came up
on the black water of the house, they found it
by the side of her bed, its pages scorched,
a layer of them arched, the corners furled
like the tips of wings, a messenger
from the other world, the solitary heart.
Did the reporter have to buy it from someone or just
pick it up and print it, so in one
day she lost her breath, her flesh
to the bone, and her secrets, each classmate read
I saw him today
be is so cute
to me on the front page, the asbestos
glove holding the small tome open
next to her school photo: ledge of her
bangs with their ring of light, one eye
looking up at each of us
who buys a paper and lifts her, one

looking over our shoulder, at the sky,
seeing its coiled strata, its swirls
of oil, its shales and coals, its veins
of carbon, as if she sees it, the heavens
solid with the ashes of the earth – heaven
had been the *earth*.

COOL BREEZE

You talked to me a lot about your kid sister,
Rebecca, a.k.a. Reebabecka,
and you knew me as my sister's kid sister,
fourteen, and a late bloomer, and homely,
you talked to me about your family,
and your dream of cutting an LP,
and the Juniors and Sophomores you were in love with, or who
were in love with you, or who maybe you had even slept with –
they were White, as I was, but you called me Miss Shary
Crobb, Miss Cool Breeze Herself.
You didn't mind I was in love with you,
you were Senior Class President.
And you would dance with me, astronomer
who pointed out to me the star
bright of the cervix, when we danced it became
exact to me, far inside
in the night sky. And you would park with me,
you would draw my hand gently across you, you had
mercy on me, and on yourself. When you would
slide your hand up under my sweater,
my mouth would open, but I would stop you, and you
would say, rather fondly, Protecting your sacred
virginity? And I would say Yes,
I could always tell you the truth.
When the White cops broke up the dance in your neighbourhood,
your friends worked to get us out the back
unseen, if the cops saw us together
they would hit someone. We crouched behind a hedge,
and I began to understand
you were less safe than me. Squatting
and whispering, I understood, as if
the bending of our bodies was teaching me,
that everyone was against you – the ones I had called

everyone, the White men
and the White women, the grown-ups, the blind
and deaf. And when you died, your LP cut,
and you had married the beauty from your neighbourhood,
when you went off the coast road with your White
lover, into the wind off the ocean,
your Jag end over end, catching
fire – I knew that my hands were not free of your
blood, brother – Reebabecka's brother.

COMING OF AGE, 1966

When I came to sex in full, not sex
by fits and starts, but day and night,
when I lived with him, I thought I would go crazy
with shock and awe. In Latin class,
my jaw would go slack, when I would remember
the night, the morning, the in, the out, the
in, the long torso of the beloved
lowered lifted lowered. When he wasn't
there, when he worked 36 On,
8 Off, 36 On, 8 Off,
I'd sit myself down to memorise Latin
so as not to go mad – my brain felt
like a planet gone oval, wobbling out of
orbit, pulling toward a new ellipsis,
I learned a year of Latin in a month,
aced the test, made love, wept, when he was
working all night I'd believe that a burglar might be
climbing the wall outside my window,
palm to the stone rosette, toe on the
granite frond, like the prowler who'd scaled the first
storey next door, been peeled from the wall
and kicked in the head. And every time
I tried to write of the body's gifts,
the child with her clothes burned off by napalm
ran into the poem screaming. I was
a Wasp child of the suburbs, I felt
cheated by Lyndon Johnson, robbed of my
entrance into the erotic, my birthright
of ease and pleasure. I understood almost
nothing of the world, but I knew that I was
connected to the girl running, her arms
out to the sides, like a plucked heron, I was
responsible for her, and helpless to reach her,

83

like the man on the sidewalk, his arms up
around his head, and all I did
was memorise Latin, and make love, and sometimes
march, my heart aching with righteousness.

What happened to her? As long as it was she,
what did she see? Strapped in,
tilted back, so her back was toward
the planet she was leaving, feeling the Gs
press her with their enormous palm, did she
weep with excitement in the roar, and in
the lens of a tear glimpse for an instant
a disc of fire? If she were our daughter,
I would probably dream how she had died, was she
torn apart, was she burned – the way
I have wondered about the first seconds
of our girl's life, when she was a cell
a cell had just entered, she hung in me
a ball of bright liquid, without nerves,
without eyes or memory, it was
she, I love her. So I want to slow it
down, and take each millisecond
up, take her, at each point,
in my mind's arms – the first, final
shock hit, as if God touched
her brain with a thumb and it went out, like a mercy killing,
and then, when it was no longer she,
the flames came – as we burned my father
when he had left himself. Then the massive bloom un-
buckled and jumped, she was vaporised back
down to the level of the cell. And the spirit –
I have never understood the spirit,
all I know is the shape it takes,
the wavering flame of flesh. Those
who know about the spirit may tell you
where she is, and why. What I want
to do is to find every cell,
slip it out of the fishes' mouths,

ash in the tree, soot in our eyes
where she enters our lives, I want to play it
backwards, burning jigsaw puzzle
of flesh suck in its million stars
to meet, in the sky, boiling metal
fly back
together, and cool.
Pull that rocket
back down
surely to earth, open the hatch
and draw them out like fresh-born creatures,
sort them out, family by family, go
away, disperse, do not meet here.

TO MY HUSBAND

At their wedding service, outdoors, the young bridesmaids'
dresses midnight-eggplant, grosgrain
satin shot with glints of maroon like
pheasant harvested, painted, and eaten,
the minister read Paul's letter to the Corinthians,
describing you. After the service
your high-school sweetheart talked about you,
your steadfastness, your kindness. She met you
a month after your mother had died
on a distant island, and every Friday and
Saturday night you went dancing, the only
teenagers on some wooden floor in some
club, holding each other, turning,
1958, 1959 . . .
Then, I understood – if it had been
half a generation later
you would have been lovers, you would have married,
and it seems to me I might be dead by now,
dead long since, not married, or married
badly, never had children or written any
words. I'd have died on West 12th Street, that time,
making a bomb – badly – they would have
identified me by my little finger, my
mother sitting in the precinct, holding
my cocked pinky.

THE SPOUSES WAKING UP
IN THE HOTEL MIRROR

The man looked like himself, only more so,
his face lucent, his silence deep as if
inevitable, but the woman looked
like a different species from an hour before,
a sandhill crane or a heron, her eyes
skinned back, she looked insane with happiness.
After he got up, I looked at her,
lying on her back in the bed.
Her ribs and breasts and clavicles had
the molded look of a gladiator's
torso-armour, formal bulge of the
pectoral, forged nipple, her deltoid
heron-elongated,
I couldn't get her provenance
but the pelvic bone was wildly curled,
wrung, I could see she was a skeleton
in there, that hair on her body buoyant
though the woman was stopped completely, stilled as if
paralyzed. I looked at her face,
blood-darkened, it was a steady face,
I saw she was very good at staring
and could make up her mind to stare at me
until I would look away first.
I saw her bowled, dark forehead,
her bony cheeks and jaws, I saw she could
watch her own house burn without
moving a muscle, I saw she could light
the pyre. She looked very much like her father, that
capillary-rich face, and very
much like her mother, the curlicues
at the corners of the features. She was very male
and very female,

very hermaphroditical,
I could see her in a temple, tying someone up
or being tied up, or being made nothing
or making someone nothing,
I saw she was full of cruelty
and full of kindness, brimming with it –
I had known but not known this, that she was human,
she had it all inside her, all of it.
She saw me seeing that, she liked that I saw it.
A full life – I saw her living it,
then I saw her think of someone who
ignores her rather as her father ignored her,
and the clear, intransigent white of her eyes
went murky grey, the sections of her face
pulled away from each other like the continents
before they tore apart, long before they drifted.
I saw that she has been beaten, I saw her
looking away like a begging dog,
I averted my eyes, and turned my head
as the man came back, and came over to her
and came down to me, I looked into his iris
like looking at a rainstorm by moonrise, or a still
winter lake, just as its cleavages
take, or into crystal, when crystal
is forming, wet as nectar or milk
or semen, the first skein from a boy's heart.

If I were in the wheelchair next to Julia,
and I could not move, and I could not speak,
could I parallel her fierce, sexual poems
with my own, raising my eyes for *yes*
when someone with a cardboard alphabet card
eventually points to the letter that is
the first letter of the first word
of the first line of my poem? At the hospital,
I feel at home, everyone there
is any one of us, struck
by a stray bullet, or a virus, or a stroke,
or fallen in front of a subway, yet I feel somehow
safe, there. Suddenly,
I understand what I am saying: the patients
cannot move, they are paralysed
as if tied up, they could not hit me.
I have trusted only the helpless, and the only
voices I cannot bear not
to hear are those of the mute, since I was
not allowed, some days, to speak
and yet I speak – look, I walk, I'm like
a titan, at the hospital, as my parents were titans
to me when they had tied me to the chair.
Do you see me now, Julia?
When I see the buds of the morning glory
I see your forearms spiralled up
toward your face, your legs on the wheelchaise
with their integrity, like pulled-up roots.
When your daughter was born, your stroke took you
and threw you off the pinnacle.
I wanted to pick up my mother when she hit me
and hurl her down on rocks. When I touch you,

it is partly her blow, upside down
and inside out, but I am not entirely
blind, Julia, I also see
you, arrow of eros, once a deer-hunter.

YOU KINDLY

Because I felt too weak to move
you kindly moved for me, kneeling
and turning, until you could take my breast-tip in the
socket of your lips, and my womb went down
on itself, drew sharply over and over
to its tightest shape, the way, when newborns
nurse, the fist of the uterus
with each, milk, tug, powerfully
shuts. I saw your hand, near me, your
daily hand, your thumbnail,
the quiet hairs on your fingers – to see your
hand its ordinary self, when your mouth at my
breast was drawing sweet gashes of come
up from my womb made black fork-flashes of a
celibate's lust shoot through me. And I couldn't
lift my head, and you swivelled, and came down
close to me, delicate blunt
touch of your hard penis in long
caresses down my face, species
happiness, calm which gleams
with fearless anguished desire. It found
my pouring mouth, the back of my throat,
and the bright wall which opens. It seemed to
take us hours to move the bone
creatures so their gods could be fitted to each other,
and then, at last, home, root
in the earth, wing in the air. As it finished,
it seemed my sex was a grey flower
the colour of the brain, smooth and glistening,
a complex calla or iris which you
were creating with the errless digit
of your sex. But then, as it finished again,
one could not speak of a blossom, or the blossom

was stripped away, as if, until
that moment, the cunt had been clothed, still,
in the thinnest garment, and now was bare
or more than bare, silver wet-suit of
matter itself gone, nothing
there but the paradise flay. And then
more, that cannot be told – may be,
but cannot be, things that did not
have to do with me, as if some
wires crossed, and history
or war, or the witches possessed, or the end
of life were happening in me, or I was
in a borrowed body, I knew
what I could not know, did-was-done-to
what I cannot do-be-done-to, so when
we returned, I cried, afraid for a moment
I was dead, and had got my wish to come back,
once, and sleep with you, on a summer
afternoon, in an empty house
where no one could hear us.
I lowered the salt breasts of my eyes
to your mouth, and you sucked,
then I looked at your face, at its absence of unkindness,
its giving that absence off as a matter
I cannot name, I was seeing not you
but something that lives between us, that can live
only between us. I stroked back the hair in
pond and sex rivulets
from your forehead, gently raked it back
along your scalp,
I did not think of my father's hair
in death, those oiled paths, I lay
along your length and did not think how he
did not love me, how he trained me not to be loved.

WHERE WILL LOVE GO?

Where will love go? When my father
died, and my love could no longer shine
on the oily, drink-darkened slopes of his skin,
then my love for him lived inside me,
and lived wherever the fog they made of him
coiled like a spirit. And when I die
my love for him will live in my vapour
and live in my children, some of it
still rubbed into the grain of the desk my father left me
and the dark-red pores of the leather chair which he
sat in, in a stupor, when I was a child, and then
gave me passionately after his death – our
souls seem locked in it, together,
two alloys in a metal, and we're there
in the black and silver workings of his 40-pound
1932 Underwood,
the trapezes stilled inside it on the desk
in front of the chair. Even when the children
have died, our love will live in their children
and still be here in the arm of the chair,
locked in it, like the secret structure of matter,

but what if we ruin everything,
the earth burning like a human body,
storms of soot wreathing it
in permanent winter? Where will love go?
Will the smoke be made of animal love,
will the clouds of roasted ice, circling
the globe, be all that is left of love,
will the sphere of cold, turning ash,
seen by no one, heard by no one,
hold all
our love? Then love
is powerless, and means nothing.

LIGHT

THE PROTESTOR

for Bob Stein

We were driving north, through the snow, you said
you had turned 21 during Vietnam, you were
1-A. The road curved
and curved back, the branches laden,
you said you had decided not to go
to Canada. Which meant you'd decided
to go to jail, a slender guy of
21, which meant you'd decided to be
raped rather than to kill, if it was their
life or your ass, it was your ass.
We drove in silence, such soft snow
so heavy borne-down. That was when I'd come to
know I loved the land of my birth –
when the men had to leave, they could never come back,
I looked and loved every American
needle on every American tree, I thought
my soul was in it. But if I were taken and
used, taken and used, I think
my soul would die, I think I'd be easily broken,
the work of my life over. And you'd said
This is the work of my life, to say,
with my body itself, You fuckers you cannot
tell me who to kill. As if there were a
spirit free of the body, safe from it.
After a while, you talked about your family,
not starting, as I had, with
husband and kids, leaving everyone else out –
you started with your grandparents
and worked your way back, away from yourself,
deeper and deeper into Europe, the Torah
buried sometimes in the garden, sometimes
swallowed and carried in the ark of the body itself.

THE FALLS

He reached out
a long arm
and grasped the hem of my undershirt.
It seemed to happen slowly, almost
casually,
the small child, floating away
from the shore of the river, the father angling
an elegant, arm, out, and hooking
the tail-tip of her undershirt
just before she enters the vector
that draws to the center, and hurtles to the head
of the falls. We were in a river in the air,
a celestial river – I did not know,
yet, that they hated each other, and the current
whisked my feet up off the bottom, I
began to make
my own way
away from the family, and my father stretched
a shapely, lean arm, and plucked me
back. I don't know if the Falls was
Yosemite or Bridalveil
or Nevada, but I could have been
their middle child who died. I would have
bobbed to the middle and been rushed to the convex
edge of the world. And then, in a braid of
whitewater and of crushive air
gone down to the roar. It shocks me how glad
I am that her mouth did not fill with water,
her heartbeat stop
mid-falls
in shock, her shin-bone, her ulna, patella,
coccyx, crack, I love her little
skull, I cherish it, I caress it

with my palm. And I love that young father
who easily, slowly, snatched her back
to her place, dead centre in that family.
No one would have written of them.
They would have died unsung – and they would have
preferred that, but my sperm king
fished me back, and gave me to my mother
to strip and towel-dry, to burnish.

THEN

And then, I opened my eyes, and saw you,
and the sight of your bone structure, and of the housing of
   your brain
brought it on so hard my whole
head distorted, as if I were seeing
love's visage. And I don't care that I'm not only
sweet, then, I always knew that I was
terrible, and I am terrible,
eyes peeled back. At the end, we sound
nearly afraid, as if we have been running
away, and this is the great catching,
the caterwauling, the nurseryful
the moment before the milk. And then
the hot edge, of the milk, and the gasps
of the milk. And then, at the centre of life,
before I exist, almost before
I want to, I open one eye. Yours
are shut, your skin is grey, your lower
jaw thrust out, you look as if you've nearly
died, or your death this instant still stands
off to one side, in full sight.
And then I know, for the first time, that we are
equals, when I see you so undone,
when I see you in the presence of final things,
blanched in vow-light. I see that you
will die, like me, and like me you are alone
on earth, you're related to the grey eel
as I am. Your skin has the eerie tint
of the early foetus, like the two we brought in,
like this, behind my innermost knot,
which slips, and cinches again, to see you
barely returned, one who has been taken
down to the ground, and below the ground,

to the world underneath it, as if my body
were a grave, and you went down into it,
and wrestled us out, and brought us back.
It is so moving to look at you,
beloved who has given himself,
holding nothing back but his gaze
which he gives, now; and now, for an hour,
the sating by gaze, and by fainting gaze,
in the chamber through which the gods do not,
for a moment, stop stalking.

THESE DAYS

Whenever I see large breasts
on a small woman, these days, my mouth
drops open, slightly.
If she's walking down the street, toward me,
it's a little painful to let her pass,
once, I heard myself, very quietly,
moan. And on the train, that time –
she couldn't have been much more than twenty,
tall and willowy – the motion of the train
jiggled her breasts steadily
like two full panfuls of water, I watched them
slosh in their tight skins, and a great
sadness came over me. I am so
tired, and thirsty. I want to suck
sweet, lacteal heat, with the savoury
silk of the human woman along
my cheek. I want to be a baby,
I want to be small and naked, or with
a dry diaper, in fond arms
with the nipple in my mouth – to work it, gently,
in its lax, nursing state, with my gums –
I do not want teeth, not even the day
stars of teeth-to-be, I want
to be soft bone, bendable,
a creature who has come out of the womb
maybe not days before,
but a couple of weeks, I want to be a capable baby,
conscious of bliss, of the nourishment
streaming out of the breast like the music
of the spheres. And I don't
want it to be
my mother. I want to start over.

ELECTRICITY SAVIOUR

He jumps up from supper, turns off the light
and returns to his place, his face flushed,
we eat our grey corn and meat.
Later, he patrols the house, sections of it
darken, abruptly, he comes into my room
and turns off the second bulb over my page.
For a while we live in partial dusk,
banging our shins, and every time
we bring the old chandelier up
to half-blaze, a wiry arm
bends around the doorframe. He knows and believes
that a continent could die. We must let the generators
sleep, as we get to lie down and sleep,
he jerks with last-second impulses
as he falls out. The next evening,
in the halls, he flits at his ease, races
and stops and slips around doorjambs to spy,
his father in a wasteful pool,
his mother in another, his sister shut
in her room with her hoarding of power, a rim
of squandered wattage pouring from around
her door. The whole family except
this boy seems willing to use the world up.
He covers it with his cloak, he holds it
to his chest, like a lamp.

SSSHH

There was someone asleep in the next room,
so my mouth was pressed shut, what was happening seemed
to be happening through me, not to me,
though in me, but to our species, or through it
to some other, as if I were a message conveyor,
a flesh Morse, which did not even
seem to be sending love, but, within the
certainty of love, to be sending the pure
specifications of the womb, indigo
and vase-shaped, or the duration and strength
of its pulses, as if that swallowing throat
could appear, now, were appearing, now,
in some other world. I lay along him,
face-down on love's uncrushable
garden, sweet odour and whisker
of earth. Where does it come from when it rises
again, using you to the perimeters,
to the air around the scalp, making
you testify, agony-mouthed – you hold
hard to the beloved as if that will save you,
it saves you, you come to, on the solid
sea of that body, it lifts you up
and down, you ride its long swell.
And then the pure joy comes,
the sheerest bliss – as if the first had been
conception; the second, birth; now
you are a living being made of this.
And now, it may be, the open eyes,
and the sight of the taper of his sulcus, that shape
of loving gaze, brings it on,
and now the hour of the bestial masks
seen. I feel his seeing of them drive
its tremors through his hardness, now hands and bones

and face dance. You may be smiling while the gnarlings
cross your smile with their diagonal distorts,
then kissing, while the waves pass through
and crinkle head and mouth. The last
minutes — I almost want to draw
a curtain around them, as if they are
invisible, or seeing would warp
the ripple of the kissings and crossings
so it could not be said. Perhaps the end
is unspeakable,
but here, where we have come, past doubt,
through into love in the face of death,
I did not cry out as it approached, I looked
and looked at him, as if calm, a direct
fearless look, straight from the cunt,
a look that is the cunt looking through the
eye, the soul looking through the cunt
through the eye in love as coming travels
stately wrenching through, like a message
sent by matter, through us, to spirit,
but who is there to hear it, only
the lovers, and now the paper whisper,
ssshh, ssshh.

THE SUMMER-CAMP BUS PULLS
AWAY FROM THE CURB

Whatever he needs, he has or doesn't
have by now.
Whatever the world is going to do to him
it has started to do. With a pencil and two
Hardy Boys and a peanut-butter sandwich and
grapes he is on his way, there is nothing
more we can do for him. Whatever is
stored in his heart, he can use, now.
Whatever he has laid up in his mind
he can call on. What he does not have
he can lack. The bus gets smaller and smaller, as one
folds a flag at the end of a ceremony,
onto itself, and onto itself, until
only a heavy wedge remains.
Whatever his exuberant soul
can do for him, it is doing right now.
Whatever his arrogance can do
it is doing to him. Everything
that's been done to him, he will now do.
Everything that's been placed in him
will come out, now, the contents of a trunk
unpacked and lined up on a bunk in the underpine light.

THE TALKERS

All week, we talked. We talked
in the morning on the porch, when I combed my hair
and flung the comb-hair out into the air,
and it floated down the slope, toward the valley.
We talked while walking to the car, talked
over its mild, belled roof,
while opening the doors, then ducked down
and there we were, bent toward the interior, talking.
Meeting, in the middle of the day,
the first thing when we saw each other
we opened our mouths. All day,
we sang to each other the level music
of spoken language. Even while we ate
we did not pause, I'd speak to him through
the broken body of the butter cookie,
gently spraying him with crumbs. We talked
and walked, we leaned against the opposite sides of the
car and talked in the parking lot
until everyone else had driven off, we clung to its
dark cold raft and started a new subject.
We did not talk about his wife, much,
or my husband, but to everything else
we turned the workings of our lips and tongues
– up to our necks in the hot tub, or
walking up the steep road,
stepping into the hot dust as if
down into the ions of a wing, and on the
sand, next to each other, as we turned
the turns that upon each other would be the
turnings of joy – even under
water there trailed from our mouths the delicate
chains of our sentences. But mostly at night, and
far into the night, we talked until we

dropped, as if, stopping for an instant, we might
move right toward each other. Today,
he said he felt he could talk to me forever,
it must be the way the angels live,
sitting across from each other, deep
in the bliss of their shared spirit. My God,
they are not going to touch each other.

SOMETIMES

And then, sometimes, you have come many times
and you feel you can't stop, and he doesn't want you to stop,
in the sombre radiance he almost laughs,
and you can hear him hum, with a bass purr, you
think he may be smiling, or he'll groan a groan in a
gasp, almost coming himself, but he
wants this to go on and on, love
dancing outside time – and, then,
it seems it may never end, you grow
directionless, you have fallen into
some centre of pleasure, you can no longer
leave and come back, you come again
without having left, you are no longer,
ever, driving wildly toward it,
you *are* it, one who does this, as if you could
lose everything else, here –
if you were not sealed in bliss, feeling
complete, you could be exhausted, lost,
as if nothing would point you home, as if
this were your home,
purposeless, as if each net
of undoing throbs were one pulse of what had
no beginning or end. You fall into it
for an afternoon, and only those sounds of
love, and that loving touch – like a family
picnic, at a distance, which a hermit hears
behind the pine boughs – keep you from despair.

FIRST THANKSGIVING

When she comes back, from college, I will see
the skin of her upper arms, cool,
matte, glossy. She will hug me, my old
soupy chest against her breasts,
I will smell her hair! She will sleep in this apartment,
her sleep like an untamed, good object,
like a soul in a body. She came into my life the
second great arrival, after him, fresh
from the other world – which lay, from within him,
within me. Those nights, I fed her to sleep,
week after week, the moon rising,
and setting, and waxing – whirling, over the months,
in a slow blur, around our planet.
Now she doesn't need love like that, she has
had it. She will walk in glowing, we will talk,
and then, when she's fast asleep, I'll exult
to have her in that room again,
behind that door! As a child, I caught
bees, by the wings, and held them, some seconds,
looked into their wild faces,
listened to them sing, then tossed them back
into the air – I remember the moment the
arc of my toss swerved, and they entered
the corrected curve of their departure.

AT THE BAY

At four in the morning, the waning crescent
rose. It still seemed full night,
Pegasus shining. The tide was low,
a clump of seaweed on the foreshore shimmered
so slightly that I had to gaze aside
to see it. The constellations were moving
up from the east. The clump glittered
in a different place – it was a snowy egret,
hunting, at the liquid edge
in the dark. I felt like a man who watches
a goddess bathe, diminutive and naked
in a clearing. The first, dawn light
seemed to come from inside the ocean,
a glow the sky picked up. Low
over the inlet, into this quiet,
a pelican flew, coming to rest
on the glossy surface. And another pelican
alighted, and the two floated
under the gold moon, in silence.
And the great blue came stalking, snake
neck and mallet beak, segment-
walking on fleshless legs at the end
of night. The air was soft and cold.
The water was smooth. Up from within it,
moving from west to east, a dolphin's
dark, back, slowly, curved.
Moments later, in the same place,
but now from east to west, it came up
past me again, and down, as if
the earth had said, I will say it twice,
Sharon, the first time backwards, to get you
ready, the second time left to right, so you can read it.

THE NATIVE

This touching of him, on the borders of sleep,
my sternum and hip-bones fitted to his tapered
back, my lap curled to his buttocks,
folded around them like a wing with an umber
eye-spot,
it feels to me like the most real thing,
my hand like elements on him, like
the waters stroking along him inside
his mother, without language, his large
eyes unsated ungrieving not even conscious yet,
the wind traveling the contours of the world,
a wind that comes when those who loved
the dead are allowed to touch them again. This feels like
who I am, I am the caressing of him,
and maybe especially this caressing,
gentle sweeping at the borders of sex,
sweeper of its sills in half-sleep, I
am the curve of his buttock, supple fork-
lightning of each hair, follicle and
pore, and underlying bone, the
death-god of the skeleton,
and the intricate, thrilling anus, like a
character on a landscape, knob-end
of one of the long drool-bones of the spirit
running the length of the body, and then –
but when we cross from the back of the body
under, then this is over, till the next
morning or night when it is back again,
my home, colourless bliss, which I quietly
walk. I saw it in the Bible, in a sideways
oval, black and white, the hills
of the peaceable kingdom, its stream and live-oak,
my eyes strolled it, and now my hand

walks, to and fro in the earth
and up and down in it, I am opposite-
Satan, I do not want to rule,
only to praise. I think I did not
want to be born,
I did not want to be conceived,
I held to nothing, to its dense parental
fur. Slowly I was pulled away,
but I would not let go, perhaps they had to
knock me off with a stick like someone
clinging to a live, downed wire,
I came away with the skin of the other
world on my palms, and at night, when I touch him,
wander on him, hold to him, and move
on and hold to him, I feel I am home again.

THE SHORE

The water was clear, grey-green, when I dove
under, it was shimmering. I looked up,
and saw a wave, passing over,
a gray bar, hurled flat toward the beach,
parallel to it, like a stone yardstick.
I went down inside, to see it again –
wild, shadowy rolling-pin
hurtling toward shore. Looking up,
without breath, and seeing it,
I felt I was in a nucleus,
seeing the forms of glisten accruing
around me in a cell. And in bed, when I,
your aqueous humour blurred a moment – not
with tears – with the blur of birth and death, and from with-
in my soul, I saw in your eye-crypt
and meshwork, the pure sea. And then,
when you, your pupil swelled, grew
and grew like a time-lapse flower in the dark on the
screen – bud, half-blossom, blossom, then the
full bloom, stretching as if it were
coming toward me, the one who dwells at your
core rising, and coming out
to me. When I cried, each tear made a shining rough
mark on you, like a rip in matter
through to spirit, and, clasped as we were, I
felt each
drop hit
and its tiny waves vibrate out, then
what we had become lay, without moving
or speaking, and then eased out, into its sleep.

THE KNOWING

Afterwards, when we have slept, paradise-
comaed, and woken, we lie a long time
looking at each other.
I do not know what he sees, but I see
eyes of quiet evenness
and endurance, a patience like the dignity
of matter. I love the open ocean
blue-grey-green of his iris, I love
the curve of it against the white,
that curve the sight of what has caused me
to go over, when he's quite still, deep
inside me. I have never seen a curve
like that, except our sphere, from outer
space. I don't know where he got
his kindness without self-regard,
almost without self, and yet
he chose one woman, instead of the others.
By knowing him, I get to know
the purity of the animal
which mates for life. Sometimes he is slightly
smiling, but mostly he just gazes at me gazing,
his entire face lit. I love
to see it change if I cry – there is no worry,
no pity, a graver radiance. If we
are on our backs, side by side,
with our faces turned fully to face each other,
I can hear a tear from my lower eye
hit the sheet, as if it is an early day on earth,
and then the upper eye's tears
braid and sluice down through the lower eyebrow
like the invention of farming, irrigation, a non-nomadic people.
I am so lucky that I can know him.
This is the only way to know him.

I am the only one who knows him.
When I wake again, he is still looking at me,
as if he is eternal. For an hour
we wake and doze, and slowly I know
that though we are sated, though we are hardly
touching, this is the coming that the other
brought us to the edge of – we are entering,
deeper and deeper, gaze by gaze,
this place beyond the other places,
beyond the body itself, we are making
love.